Mandalas for Relaxation and Creativity: Flowers from Colombia

Amarela

ISBN: 979-8-9893233-1-9

Welcome to "Mandalas for Relaxation and Creativity: Flowers from Colombia," a captivating coloring book that invites you to embark on a vibrant journey through the enchanting world of Colombian flowers. In this book, you'll discover a collection of intricately designed mandalas inspired by the breathtaking flora of Colombia, a country renowned for its rich biodiversity and stunning floral diversity.

Immerse yourself in the therapeutic and meditative art of coloring mandalas as you bring these exquisite floral designs to life. Each page offers a unique opportunity to relax, unwind, and reconnect with your inner creativity. Whether you're an experienced artist or simply seeking a moment of tranquility, this coloring book is a perfect companion.

Discover 48 Custom Mandalas

Transport yourself with the enchanting beauty of 12 different types of Colombian flowers, each adorned with 4 unique mandalas, totaling an astounding 48 distinct designs.

A Canvas of Inspiration

Every petal, every curve, and every color have a story to tell. Within these mandalas, you'll find more than just patterns to color. Each type of flower reveals a world of inspiration:

- **Famous Flower Quotes**: Unearth the wisdom of poets, writers, and thinkers who have been inspired by the elegance of flowers.
- **Mandalas of Transformation**: Embark on a journey of self-discovery with quotes that illuminate the transformative power of mandalas in your life.
- **Floral Facts**: Delve into fascinating facts about each flower, unveiling the secrets of their unique characteristics and significance.
- **Haiku Harmony**: Savor the elegance of a haiku, a form of Japanese poetry, crafted to capture the essence of each flower in just a few lines.

How to Embark on Your Coloring Journey

1. **Choose Your Mandalas**: Select a mandala that resonates with your mood, and let your creativity bloom.
2. **Colors of Imagination**: Gather your favorite coloring tools, from vibrant pens and markers to soothing colored pencils.
3. **Relax and Reflect**: Find a tranquil space, play soft music, and let the stresses of the day melt away as you dive into the world of Colombian floral beauty.
4. **Color with Intent**: Allow each stroke to be a mindful experience, and let the colors flow, taking you on a journey of self-expression.
5. **Share Your Masterpiece**: Share your colored mandalas with friends and family, or keep them as a personal testament to your creativity.

ACACALLIS CYANEA
ORCHID

"THE LANGUAGE OF FLOWERS NEEDS NO TRANSLATION."
- GILDA RADNER

ACACALLIS CYANEA ORCHID

EACH MANDALA IS A UNIQUE EXPRESSION
OF THE INDIVIDUAL'S INNER ESSENCE.

ACACALLIS CYANEA
ORCHID

ORCHID FLOWERS ARE SYMMETRICAL.
EACH FLOWER CAN BE PERFECTLY DIVIDED IN HALF,
INTO TWO EQUAL PARTS.

ACACALLIS CYANEA ORCHID

ORCHID'S GENTLE GRACE
HIDES THE SECRETS OF ITS HEART,
NATURE'S CRYPTIC ART.

BEGONIA

"FLOWERS ARE THE CONSTELLATIONS OF THE EARTH."
- DOROTHY PARKER

BEGONIA

IN THE MANDALA, WE FIND THE UNITY OF
THE SELF AND THE COSMOS.

BEGONIA

MANY BEGONIAS ARE EDIBLE AND ARE A GREAT SOURCE OF
VITAMIN C. THE STEMS OF BEGONIAS ARE SIMILAR TO RHUBARB
BOTH IN TASTE AND TEXTURE.

BEGONIA

WITHIN THE STILLNESS,
BEGONIA STIRS WITH GRACE,
SOULFUL HUES EMERGE.

BIRDS OF PARADISE

"FLOWERS ARE THOUGHTS OF NATURE."
- PHILIP MILLER

BIRDS OF PARADISE

MANDALAS REMIND US OF THE
INTERCONNECTEDNESS OF ALL LIFE.

BIRDS OF PARADISE

THE BIRD OF PARADISE IS KNOWN AS A SYMBOL OF
PARADISE, FREEDOM, AND GOOD FORTUNE.

BIRDS OF PARADISE

LEAVES LIKE FANS UNFOLD,
BIRD OF PARADISE, STORY TOLD,
BEAK AND HEAD, BEHOLD.

BLAZING STAR

"FLOWERS ARE THE POETRY OF THE EARTH."
- RALPH WALDO EMERSON

BLAZING STAR

THE MANDALA IS A SYMBOL OF WHOLENESS,
COMPLETENESS, AND INTEGRATION.

BLAZING STAR

NATIVE AMERICAN TRIBES USED PARTS OF THE PLANT FOR
MEDICINAL PURPOSES, INCLUDING TREATING TOOTHACHES
AND SKIN CONDITIONS.

BLAZING STAR

BLAZING STAR'S BRIEF REIGN
IN FIELDS, A COLORFUL STAIN,
IN SUN AND IN RAIN.

CHRISTMAS ORCHID

"THE BEAUTY OF A FLOWER UNFOLDS IN ITS OWN TIME."
- MATSHONA DHLIWAYO

CHRISTMAS ORCHID

THROUGH MANDALAS, WE CAN BRING ORDER
TO THE CHAOS OF OUR INNER WORLD.

CHRISTMAS ORCHID

CULTIVATING AN ORCHID REQUIRES PATIENCE.
THE PLANT'S FIRST FLOWERS MAY NOT APPEAR UNTIL
5 TO 7 YEARS AFTER GERMINATION.

CHRISTMAS ORCHID

ORCHID'S GENTLE CURVE,
IN ITS PRESENCE, WE OBSERVE,
NATURE'S TENDER FACE.

COLOMBIAN ROSE

"THE LANGUAGE OF FLOWERS IS THE SILENT LANGUAGE OF LOVE."
- MAX MULLER

COLOMBIAN ROSE

THE MANDALA IS A MIRROR REFLECTING
THE HARMONY OF THE UNIVERSE.

COLOMBIAN ROSE

THE FRAGRANCE OF A ROSE EMANATES FROM THE
TINY GLANDS HIDDEN IN ITS LOWER PETALS, AS IF THEY WERE
PERFUMED SECRETS KEPT NEAR ITS HEART.

COLOMBIAN ROSE

THORNS MAY GUARD ITS PARTS,
YET THE ROSE IMPARTS ITS ART,
IN AIR AND THE HEART.

GERANIUM

"FLOWERS ARE LIKE FRIENDS;
THEY BRING COLOR TO YOUR WORLD."
- ANONYMOUS

GERANIUM

MANDALAS HELP US TAP INTO OUR
CREATIVE POTENTIAL AND INNER WISDOM.

GERANIUM

GERANIUM LEAVES CONTAIN ESSENTIAL OILS THAT HUMANS FIND PLEASANT
IN SCENT. HOWEVER, FOR INSECTS LIKE MOSQUITOES AND WASPS,
IT'S A NATURAL DETERRENT.

GERANIUM

GERANIUM'S HUE
A BURST OF COLOR SO TRUE,
ENERGY FLOWS THROUGH.

HELICONIA

"FLOWERS ARE THE SHOOTING STARS OF THE EARTH."
- MATSHONA DHLIWAYO

HELICONIA

MANDALAS ARE A TOOL FOR INNER TRANSFORMATION AND GROWTH.

HELICONIA

HELICONIA'S ABILITY TO WITHSTAND HARSH WEATHER CONDITIONS
AND STILL BLOOM BEAUTIFULLY IS REGARDED AS A METAPHOR FOR
OVERCOMING LIFE'S CHALLENGES AND ADVERSITY WITH GRACE.

HELICONIA

AMIDST JUNGLE'S GREEN,
HELICONIA'S VIVID FLAME,
A SHINING LIGHT SEEN.

LADY'S SLIPPER ORCHID

"IN EVERY FLOWER, THERE IS A SOUL,
AND IN EVERY SOUL, A WORLD."
- G. K. CHESTERTON

LADY'S SLIPPER ORCHID

MANDALAS ARE A MAP OF THE SOUL'S JOURNEY
TOWARDS INDIVIDUATION.

LADY'S SLIPPER ORCHID

LADY'S SLIPPER ORCHIDS ARE LIKE LITTLE ARTISTIC REBELS
EACH ONE HAS ITS OWN STYLE, FROM PETAL SHAPE TO COLOR
INTENSITY. THAT'S WHAT MAKES THEM SO CHARMINGLY UNIQUE.

LADY'S SLIPPER ORCHID

ELEGANCE CONCEALED,
GRACE IN A HIDDEN BALLET,
LADY'S SLIPPER SWAYS.

MIDNIGHT JASMINE

"JASMINE REMINDS US THAT EVEN IN DARKNESS,
THERE IS BEAUTY TO BE FOUND."
- UNKNOWN

MIDNIGHT JASMINE

MANDALAS ARE THE LANGUAGE OF THE SOUL,
REVEALING ITS DEEPEST TRUTHS.

MIDNIGHT JASMINE

JASMINE UNVEILS ITS FRAGRANCE UNDER THE VEIL OF NIGHT,
ESPECIALLY WHEN THE MOON IS WAXING TOWARD FULLNESS.

MIDNIGHT JASMINE

A NOCTURNAL FACE
MIDNIGHT JASMINE'S PETALS LACE,
A LUNAR EMBRACE.

TULIPS

"FLOWERS ARE A GIFT FROM NATURE THAT WARMS THE HEART."
- ANONYMOUS

TULIPS

COLORING MANDALAS IS A FORM OF
MEDITATION IN MOTION.

TULIPS

TULIPS CONTINUE TO GROW AND FOLLOW THE SUN
EVEN WHEN THEY'RE IN A VASE.

TULIPS

AMIDST THE GREEN SEA,
TULIPS BLOOM IN HARMONY,
SPRING'S ARTISTRY.

WAX BEGONIA

"A FLOWER DOES NOT THINK OF COMPETING WITH THE FLOWER NEXT TO IT. IT JUST BLOOMS."
- ZEN SHIN

WAX BEGONIA

EACH MANDALA IS A UNIQUE REFLECTION OF
THE INDIVIDUAL'S INNER TRUTH.

WAX BEGONIA

WAX BEGONIAS HOLD A SPECIAL PLACE AS SYMBOLS OF GOOD FORTUNE. THEY'RE CHERISHED GIFTS, OFFERED TO BESTOW PROSPERITY AND JOY.

WAX BEGONIA

IN THE SHADE THEY THRIVE,
RAIN-KISSED THEY GLISTEN AND STRIVE,
GARDEN'S SECRET HIVE.